The Best 50
PANCAKE
RECIPES

Rachel Wylde

BRISTOL PUBLISHING ENTERPRISES
Hayward, California

©2007 Bristol Publishing Enterprises
2714 McCone Ave., Hayward, California 94545.

World rights reserved. No part of this publication
may be reproduced in any form, nor may it be stored in a retrieval
system, transmitted, or otherwise copied for public or private use
without prior written permission from the publisher.

Printed in the United States of America.

ISBN-13: 978-1-55867-335-9
ISBN-10: 1-55867-335-0

Cover design:	Frank J. Paredes
Cover photography:	John A. Benson
Food stylist:	Randy Mon

A BRIEF HISTORY OF PANCAKES

Pancakes are amazing for many reasons. They have a long history; international connections; incredible variety; and broad appeal—especially to children.

Pancakes are actually a type of flatbread—in other words, bread that is made without yeast. Flatbreads are one of the oldest and most basic types of food. They were eaten by ancient peoples as far back as ancient Rome. The modern variety of pancakes were "invented" in medieval Europe. Pancake recipes have been found in cookbooks from as far back as the 13th century.

Pancakes have been pervasive throughout history and around the world because they can be made with the simplest of equipment: A grill or skillet over a small fire is all that is needed. They have been a part of social rituals for almost as long as they have existed. The most famous is Shrove Tuesday (called Fat Tuesday or Mardi Gras in the United States). Pancakes were eaten on Shrove Tuesday, the day before Lent begins, as a way to deplete stores of eggs and fat, both of which were forbidden by the Catholic Church during Lent. In the United States, pancakes are made with a leavening agent (baking powder or baking soda or both), and are also referred to as hotcakes, griddle cakes, or flapjacks.

Pancakes appear in the cuisines of almost every country: drop scones (thinner versions of regular scones) in Scotland; crêpes in France; boxty (thick potato/flour griddle cakes) in Ireland; and cannoli in Italy (pancakes fried crisp in a tube shape and then filled). One can eat both sweet and savory versions in Japan, called dorayaki and okonomiyaki respectively. In China, scallion pancakes and mu shu (thin pancakes wrapped around savory fillings) are very popular. Malaysia, Singapore, India and Vietnam each all have their versions of this versatile dish. Pita in the Middle East, injera in Ethiopia, latkes in Israel, blini in Russia and lefse in Scandanavia are other examples of the versatile pancake.

Of the many varieties of pancakes found throughout the world, it is interesting to note that there are as many salty, savory pancakes as there are sweet breakfast and dessert pancakes. These range from miniature blini topped with caviar; to crêpes filled with meat and vegetables as a main meal; to enormous sheets of Ethiopian injera that are used to scoop up mouthfuls of stews—which are in turn served on a round of injera. Not many other foods can boast this kind of variety in ethnic origin, textures and flavors.

TIPS ON COOKING YOUR PANCAKES

- When making thicker, flour-based (breakfast-style) pancakes, don't over-beat the batter once the dry ingredients have been added, or you will have a tough cake.
- Expect a few lumps in your batter; they will disappear during cooking.
- Cook the pancakes on the first side until you can see that the edges are a bit dry. You'll also see holes in the top where bubbles have formed and popped.

- Flip only once. The second side cooks faster than the first.
- Depending on the type of pan you use, you may not need to add any more butter or oil to the pan after the first batch.
- When making crêpes and thin pancakes, the batter should be smooth. Pour a small amount of batter into a hot pan and swirl immediately to spread the batter into a very thin, almost transparent, layer. Be patient: the first crêpe is often a mess, but the following ones will be fine.
- Moisture is the enemy of potato pancakes. Make sure you squeeze the grated potatoes to remove excess liquid.

When I was a child I ate pancakes whenever I could. But although I became an avid cook as a teenager, I never made pancakes until I had children of my own. They are an excellent way to introduce healthy ingredients to picky eaters. Saturday or Sunday pancake breakfasts have become a ritual in our house: it's a way to start the weekend in a relaxed and comforting way.

BASIC BUTTERMILK PANCAKES

Servings: 4

These are my basic pancakes. They are light and fluffy and their sweetness comes from the additions you choose. Try topping them with maple syrup, berries, sautéed apples, or sliced nectarines.

3/4 cup flour
1/2 tsp. salt
1 tsp. baking soda

1 egg
1 cup buttermilk
1 tbs. butter, melted

In a bowl, blend flour, salt and baking soda. In another bowl, whisk egg, buttermilk and butter together. Add egg mixture to flour mixture and stir just to combine. Batter will be lumpy.

Place a skillet over medium heat. When hot, lightly coat pan with butter. Pour 1/4 cup batter per pancake into skillet. Cook until bubbles burst on surface and undersides are golden brown, 2 to 3 minutes, then turn and cook until set and lightly browned, about 1 minute longer. Keep warm in a 200° oven while you repeat with remaining batter, adding butter to pan if necessary.

BUTTERMILK PANCAKES #2

Try these as an alternative to the Basic Buttermilk Pancakes. They are sweeter and even fluffier.

1 1/2 cups all-purpose flour or whole-wheat flour
2 tbs. sugar
1/2 tsp. salt
1 tsp. baking soda
2 tsp. baking powder
1/4 tsp. ground nutmeg
2 eggs
3 tbs. butter, melted
1 1/2 cups buttermilk
1 tsp. vanilla extract

Blend together flour, sugar, salt, baking soda, baking powder and nutmeg in a bowl. In a separate bowl, beat eggs and stir in butter, buttermilk and vanilla. Add egg mixture to flour mixture and stir just to combine. Batter will be lumpy.

Heat a skillet over medium heat. When hot, coat lightly with butter. Pour $1/4$ cup batter per pancake into skillet. Cook until bubbles burst on surface and undersides are golden brown, 2 to 3 minutes, then turn and cook until set and lightly browned, about 1 minute longer. Don't pat them or flip them again, or pancakes will become heavy. Keep warm in a 200° oven while you repeat with remaining batter, adding butter to pan if necessary.

BASIC WHOLE-WHEAT PANCAKES

Servings: 4

Whole wheat flour is lighter than many other whole-grain flours but provides a healthy alternative to white flour. Try substituting 1/2 cup oat bran for an equal amount of the flour for a nutty taste.

1 1/2 cups whole-wheat flour
1-2 tbs. sugar
1/2 tsp. salt
1 tsp. baking soda
2 tsp. baking powder
1/4 tsp. ground nutmeg
2 eggs
3 tbs. butter, melted, or oil
1 1/2 cups buttermilk
1 tsp. vanilla extract

Blend together flour, sugar, salt, baking soda, baking powder and nutmeg in a bowl. In another bowl, beat eggs and add butter, buttermilk and vanilla. Add egg mixture to flour mixture and stir just to combine. Batter will be lumpy.

Heat a skillet over medium heat. When hot, lightly coat pan with butter. Pour ¼ cup batter per pancake into skillet. Cook until bubbles burst on surface and undersides are golden brown, 2 to 3 minutes, then turn and cook until set and lightly browned, about 1 minute longer. Don't pat them or flip them again, or pancakes will become heavy. Keep warm in a 200° oven while you repeat with remaining batter, adding butter to pan if necessary.

VARIATION: WHOLE-WHEAT ALMOND PANCAKES

Use olive oil instead of butter. Substitute almond extract for vanilla extract. Top each pancake with 1 tbs. finely chopped almonds before flipping. Serve with maple syrup and sour cream or *Crème Fraîche*, page 74.

ORANGE WHOLE WHEAT PANCAKES

Servings: 4

These fruity cakes are very popular with my kids despite their healthy ingredients. If possible, use fresh-squeezed orange juice.

2 cups whole wheat flour	2 eggs
1/2 tsp salt	1/4 cup vegetable oil
1/2 tsp. baking soda	1 1/2 cups orange juice

In a bowl, blend flour, salt and baking soda. In another bowl, beat eggs and oil. Add to dry ingredients alternately with orange juice; stir just to combine. Batter will be lumpy.

Heat a skillet over medium heat. Lightly coat pan with butter. Pour 1/4 cup batter per pancake into skillet. Cook until bubbles burst on surface and undersides are golden brown, 2 to 3 minutes, then turn and cook until set and lightly browned, about 1 minute longer. Don't pat them or flip them again, or pancakes will become heavy. Serve right away, or keep warm in a 200° oven while you repeat with remaining batter, adding butter to pan if necessary.

BUCKWHEAT BACON PANCAKES

Servings: 4

These fluffy cakes get their full-bodied quality from buckwheat and Canadian bacon. They are delicious with maple syrup.

½ cup buckwheat flour
½ cup all-purpose flour
1 tsp. sugar
1 tsp. baking powder
½ tsp. baking soda

¼ tsp. salt
1 egg, lightly beaten
1¼ cups buttermilk
2 tbs. vegetable oil
¼ lb. Canadian bacon, diced

In a bowl, stir together buckwheat and all-purpose flour, sugar, baking powder, baking soda and salt. Add egg, buttermilk and oil and stir just to combine. Batter will be lumpy. Stir in bacon. Heat a skillet over medium heat and lightly coat with oil. Pour ¼ cup batter per pancake into skillet and cook, turning once, until golden, about 4 minutes total. Keep warm in a 200° oven while you repeat with remaining batter, adding oil to pan if necessary.

BUCKWHEAT BANANA-PECAN PANCAKES

Buckwheat pancakes are classic American fare, with recipes dating back to early American history. The banana caramelizes in the skillet, giving the pancakes a wonderful rich flavor. You can also make these with buttermilk batter.

1/3 cup chopped pecans
1 egg
1 cup buttermilk
1 tbs. butter, melted
1/2 cup all-purpose flour
1/4 cup buckwheat flour
1/2 tsp. salt
1 tsp. baking soda
1 large banana, sliced

Heat oven to 375°. Place pecans in a metal pie pan or on a cookie sheet. Bake until brown and fragrant, about 10 minutes. Watch to be sure they don't burn.

In a bowl, whisk egg, buttermilk and butter together. In a separate bowl, blend together flour, salt and baking soda. Stir into buttermilk mixture just to combine. Batter will be lumpy.

Heat a skillet over medium heat. When hot, lightly coat pan with butter. Pour ¼ cup batter per pancake into skillet. Place a few banana slices and pecans on each cake. Cook until bubbles burst on surface and undersides are golden brown, 2 to 3 minutes, then turn and cook until set and lightly browned, about 1 minute longer. Keep warm in a 200° oven while you repeat with remaining batter, adding butter to pan if necessary.

BUCKWHEAT PANCAKES
WITH CRANBERRY APPLESAUCE

Servings: 4

Buckwheat flour is widely used in France to make crêpes. It is an excellent flour for people who are watching their cholesterol.

1 1/4 cups all-purpose flour or whole-wheat flour	2 tsp. baking powder
1/4 cup buckwheat flour	1/4 tsp. ground nutmeg
1-2 tbs. sugar	2 eggs
1/2 tsp. salt	3 tbs. butter, melted, or oil
1 tsp. baking soda	1 1/2 cups buttermilk
	1 tsp. vanilla extract

In a bowl, blend together flours, sugar, salt, baking soda, baking powder and nutmeg. In another bowl, beat eggs and add butter, buttermilk and vanilla. Add egg mixture to flour mixture and stir just to combine. Batter will be lumpy.

Heat a skillet over medium heat. When hot, lightly coat pan with butter. Pour 1/4 cup batter per pancake into skillet. Cook until bubbles burst on surface and undersides are golden brown, 2 to 3 minutes, then turn and cook until set and lightly browned, about 1 minute longer. Don't pat or flip again, or pancakes will become heavy. Keep warm in a 200° oven while you repeat with remaining batter, adding butter to pan if necessary.

CRANBERRY APPLESAUCE

Makes about 4 cups

½ cup fresh cranberries
½ cup apple juice or water
6 large apples, peeled, cored
   and sliced, about 3 lb.

juice of 1 lemon
sugar to taste

Place cranberries and juice in a saucepan. Cover and cook over medium-low heat for 10 minutes. Add apples and cook 15 minutes longer, until quite soft, stirring as needed. Remove from heat and mash with a fork. Add lemon juice; add sugar 1 tsp. at a time to taste. Be careful not to over-sweeten. Serve warm or at room temperature. Store covered in the refrigerator.

OATMEAL PANCAKES

Servings: 4

If you're in a hurry, substitute quick-cooking oats. Or, substitute steel-cut oats and soak in the buttermilk overnight; in the morning add the remaining ingredients. Use rolled oats for the best texture, however. Serve with applesauce or sautéed apples and yogurt.

1 1/2 cups rolled oats
2 cups buttermilk
2 eggs
1 tsp. vanilla extract
2 tbs. brown sugar, packed, or maple syrup
1/4 cup canola oil
1/2 tsp. salt
1/2 cup flour
1/4 tsp. ground nutmeg
1/2 tsp. baking soda

In a bowl, stir together oats and buttermilk and soak for 20 minutes. In another bowl, beat eggs with vanilla, sugar and oil. Stir in soaked oats and any buttermilk remaining. In a small bowl, combine salt, flour, nutmeg and baking soda. Add dry ingredients to oat mixture. Place a large skillet over medium-low heat and lightly coat with oil. Pour 1/4 cup batter per pancake into skillet and cook until bubbles burst on surface and undersides are golden brown. Turn and cook until second sides are golden. Cook cakes slowly, but turn only once. Keep warm in a 200° oven while you repeat with remaining batter, adding oil to pan if necessary.

OATMEAL-BUTTERMILK PANCAKES WITH FRUIT

Gently stir a cup of blackberries, raspberries or mulberries into batter and cook as described. Serve pancakes with a mound of blackberries sweetened with brown sugar and a dollop of yogurt.

WHOLE GRAIN-BUTTERMILK PANCAKES

Servings: 4

Blackstrap molasses makes these pancakes hearty. If you prefer, you may lighten them by substituting 2 tbs. honey or light molasses. Try these wholesome cakes with fresh berries and a drizzle of honey.

1 cup whole wheat flour
1/3 cup all-purpose flour
1/3 cup quick-cooking oats
1/3 cup yellow cornmeal
2 tsp. baking powder
1/4 tsp. baking soda
1/4 tsp. salt
2 cups buttermilk
2 eggs
2 tbs. butter, melted
1 tbs. blackstrap molasses

In a bowl, blend flours, oats, cornmeal, baking powder, baking soda and salt. In another bowl, whisk buttermilk, eggs, butter and molasses. Add egg mixture to flour mixture and stir just to combine.

Heat a skillet over medium heat and lightly coat with butter. Pour 1/4 cup batter per pancake into skillet. Cook until bubbles burst on surface and undersides are golden brown, 3 minutes. Turn pancakes and cook until second sides are golden, 3 minutes longer. Keep warm in a 200° oven while you repeat with remaining batter, adding butter to pan if necessary.

MIXED-GRAIN PANCAKES

These are light and delicate and allow you the freedom to experiment with textures and flavors. Instead of the cooked grain, try ½ cup whole-grain cereal, oats or millet for a crunchy texture.

1 egg
1 cup buttermilk
1 tbs. butter, melted
½ cup all-purpose flour
½ cup cooked grain such as rice or quinoa
¼ cup cornmeal
¼ cup rye or buckwheat flour
½ tsp. salt
1 tsp. baking soda

In a bowl, whisk egg, buttermilk and melted butter together. In another bowl, blend together flour, salt and baking soda. Add egg mixture to flour mixture and stir just to combine. Batter will be lumpy.

Heat a skillet over medium heat and lightly coat pan with butter. Pour $1/4$ cup batter per pancake into skillet. Cook until bubbles burst on surface and undersides are golden brown, 2 to 3 minutes, then turn and cook until set and lightly browned, about 1 minute longer. Keep warm in a 200° oven while you repeat with remaining batter, adding butter to pan if necessary.

GLUTEN-FREE PANCAKES

Servings: 4

This recipe is a good basic pancake for people with gluten intolerance, a symptom of coeliac disease.

1 cup brown rice flour
1/2 cup potato starch flour
1/4 cup tapioca flour
1/4 cup cornstarch
1 tbs. gluten-free baking powder
1 tbs. sugar

1/4 tsp. salt
1 1/2 cups almond milk
3 eggs
4 tbs. vegetable oil
butter or margarine for cooking

In a bowl, combine flours, cornstarch, baking powder, sugar and salt. In another bowl, mix almond milk, eggs and oil. Stir mixtures together. Heat a nonstick pan over medium heat. Add butter or margarine. When pan is hot, pour 1/2 cup batter to form pancake. When the bubbles that form in pancake start turning into holes, flip pancake. Cook until golden; serve with real maple syrup.

FLUFFY EGGLESS PANCAKES

Chopped fruit or nuts can be added to this batter for a unique treat. This recipe also works well with whole wheat flour.

1 tsp. sugar
1 cup all-purpose flour
1 tsp. cinnamon
2 tsp. baking powder
1 cup whole milk

1 tbs. vegetable oil
1 tbs. water
1 tsp. vanilla extract
2 tbs. butter

Combine sugar, flour, cinnamon and baking powder and mix slightly. Add milk, oil, water and vanilla. Whisk until just combined. Be careful not to overmix—batter should be lumpy. Set aside.

Heat a large skillet over medium-high heat. Add butter. As soon as butter is melted, add to pancake batter. Return pan to stove and stir butter into batter. When pan is hot, pour ¼ cup batter for each pancake. Cook until bubbles form on the surface. Carefully flip pancakes and cook until golden brown.

LEMON RICOTTA PANCAKES

These delicate, spongy cakes are so popular, my children beg me to make them every weekend. They are low in calories and high in calcium, protein and fiber. Serve with mixed berries.

1 cup ricotta cheese, regular or part-skim
1/4 cup milk, regular or lowfat
3 eggs, separated
2 tbs. granulated sugar
1/3 cup flour
1 tbs. grated lemon zest
1/4 tsp. salt
1 pinch cream of tartar
2 tbs. confectioners' sugar

Place ricotta in a large bowl and add milk, egg yolks and granulated sugar. Whisk together until blended. Add flour, lemon zest and salt. Stir just until blended.

In another bowl, combine egg whites and cream of tartar. Using a whisk or electric mixer, beat until soft peaks form. Gently fold beaten whites into ricotta mixture, just until blended.

Heat a large skillet over medium heat and lightly coat with oil. Pour $1/3$ cup batter per pancake into skillet. Reduce heat to medium-low and cook until small bubbles appear around edges of pancakes and bottoms are lightly browned, about 2 to 3 minutes. Turn pancakes and cook until golden, 1 to 2 minutes longer. Keep warm in a 200° oven while you repeat with remaining batter, adding oil to pan if necessary. Dust pancakes with confectioners' sugar.

COTTAGE CHEESE PANCAKES

The batter for these pancakes is sticky, so add oil or butter to the pan each time. Serve with Creme Fraiche, page 74, or sour cream and strawberry jam.

1 cup flour
1/2 tsp. baking soda
1 tbs. sugar
1/4 tsp. salt
1/4 tsp. ground nutmeg
2 eggs, separated
1 cup buttermilk
1 cup cottage cheese
1/4 cup (1/2 stick) butter, melted
1 tsp. vanilla extract

In a small bowl, stir together flour, baking soda, sugar, salt and nutmeg. Whisk egg yolks and buttermilk together in a separate bowl; stir in cottage cheese, butter and vanilla. Add dry ingredients to buttermilk mixture and whisk together quickly. In a separate bowl, beat egg whites with a whisk or mixer until they form soft peaks and fold gently into batter.

Heat a skillet over medium heat. When hot, lightly coat pan with oil. Pour 1/4 cup batter per pancake into skillet. Cook until bubbles burst on top and bottom is golden, about 4 minutes, then turn and cook until set and lightly browned, about 1 minute longer. These generally take a little longer to cook than other cakes. Keep warm in a 200° oven while you repeat with remaining batter, adding oil to pan as necessary.

BUTTERMILK PANCAKES
WITH BLUEBERRY COMPOTE

Servings: 4

Sour cream and buttermilk give these a tangy flavor. The compote is easy to make, but these are also great with butter and jam.

2½ cups flour
2 tbs. sugar
2 tsp. baking powder
2 tsp. salt
2 cups buttermilk

2 cups sour cream
2 eggs
2 tsp. vanilla extract
Blueberry Compote, page 29

In a large bowl, blend flour, sugar, baking powder and salt. In another bowl, whisk buttermilk, sour cream, eggs and vanilla. Add to dry ingredients. Stir until batter is just blended but still lumpy.

Heat a skillet over medium heat and lightly coat with butter. Pour ⅓ cup batter per pancake into skillet. Cook until bubbles burst on surface and undersides are golden brown, 3 minutes. Turn pancakes over. Cook until bottoms are golden, about 3 minutes longer.

Keep warm in a 200° oven while you repeat with remaining batter, adding butter to pan if necessary. Serve pancakes with *Blueberry Compote.*

BLUEBERRY COMPOTE
Makes about 1½ cups

This is great with just about any breakfast pancake recipe, and is also a good topping for yogurt or oatmeal.

2½ cups fresh or frozen blueberries, divided

⅓ cup sugar
⅓ cup water

Combine 1½ cups of the blueberries, sugar and water in a heavy saucepan. Simmer over medium heat until berries burst, stirring often, about 10 minutes. Add remaining 1 cup berries. Cook, stirring often, until compote coats a spoon, about 8 minutes. Serve warm.

HEARTY APPLE PANCAKES
WITH RASPBERRY SAUCE

Servings: 6

These hearty pancakes involve some additional steps but they are not complicated and are well worth the effort.

2 pkg. (12 oz. each) frozen
    unsweetened raspberries,
    thawed
1 cup + 3 tbs. sugar, divided
1/4 cup water
1 tbs. Kirsch (cherry brandy)
2 cups flour
1 1/2 tsp. baking powder

3/4 tsp. baking soda
1/2 tsp. salt
2 cups buttermilk
2 eggs
6 tbs. butter, melted, divided
5 Granny Smith apples, peeled,
    cored, cut into slices
1/2 tsp. cinnamon

In a heavy saucepan over medium heat, cook berries, 2/3 cup of the sugar and water, stirring, until mixture comes to a boil. Place in a food processor workbowl and puree. Strain into a bowl, pressing on solids. Mix in Kirsch. Cover and refrigerate. Sauce can be made 1 day ahead.

Blend flour, 3 tbs. of the sugar, baking powder, baking soda and salt in a large bowl. Whisk buttermilk, eggs and 2 tbs. of the butter in a medium bowl; mix into dry ingredients. Set batter aside. In a large skillet over medium heat, heat remaining 4 tbs. butter. Add apples, cinnamon and remaining $1/3$ cup sugar; sauté until apples are golden, about 10 minutes.

Heat a large skillet over medium heat and lightly coat with butter. Pour $1/2$ cup batter into skillet, tilting to form a 7- to 8-inch-diameter pancake. Cook until golden brown on bottom, about 3 minutes. Turn and cook until brown, about 2 minutes. Place $1/6$ of the apple mixture on half of pancake; fold pancake in half. Keep warm in a 200° oven while you repeat with remaining batter, adding butter to pan if necessary. Serve pancakes with reserved raspberry sauce.

APPLE PANCAKES
WITH CINNAMON BUTTER

Servings: 4

This recipe originates from Scotland where, as in Sweden, pancakes are small and often served not at breakfast but at teatime.

½ cup (1 stick) butter, softened
½ cup confectioners' sugar
1 tsp. cinnamon
½ tsp. grated orange zest
2 tsp. fresh lemon juice
1 tsp. grated lemon zest
2 tart medium apples, peeled

1⅔ cups flour
2 tbs. brown sugar, packed
2½ tsp. baking powder
½ tsp. salt
¾ cup whole milk
2 eggs
¼ cup (½ stick) butter, melted

In a small bowl, mix soft butter, confectioners' sugar, cinnamon and orange zest until blended. Set aside.

Combine lemon juice and lemon zest in a bowl. Coarsely shred apples into bowl, tossing to coat with juice.

Whisk together flour, brown sugar, baking powder and salt in a large bowl. Make a well in center of dry ingredients. Pour milk, eggs and melted butter in the well and whisk into dry ingredients until batter is smooth. Stir in apple mixture. Cover and set aside at room temperature for at least 30 minutes or up to 1 hour.

Heat a large skillet over medium-high heat and lightly coat with butter. Pour 1 heaping tbs. batter per pancake into skillet, spacing pancakes apart. Cook until bubbles burst on surface and undersides are golden brown, about 3 minutes. Turn over and cook about 2 minutes longer, until golden. Keep warm in a 200° oven. Repeat with remaining batter, brushing skillet with butter before each batch. Serve with a dollop of reserved cinnamon butter.

APPLE OR PEAR PANCAKES

Use fresh fall apples if possible, but you can even use apples whose texture is no longer great for eating.

3 lb. apples, cored and
   quartered
½ cup water
honey or sugar to taste

fresh lemon juice, optional
½ tsp. cinnamon, cardamom or
   allspice, or 1 pinch cloves

Make the *Basic Buttermilk Pancake* batter according to instructions on page 5.

Peel, core and thinly slice 1 or 2 apples or pears and stir them into batter along with ¼ tsp. ground cardamom, cinnamon or nutmeg. Serve with maple syrup, *Applesauce, Quince Sauce,* or *Pear Sauce*, page 35.

APPLESAUCE   Makes about 1 quart

Place apples in a saucepan, add water, cover and cook until apples are completely tender, about 20 minutes. Or, in a pressure cooker with $1/4$ cup of water, bring pressure to high and cook for 10 minutes. Release pressure. Pass cooked fruit through a coarse strainer or food mill if skins are left on, or simply mash if not. Taste and season with honey, sugar or lemon juice if desired. Add spices and simmer for 5 minutes longer for flavors to blend and sauce to thicken, then cool.

QUINCE OR PEAR SAUCE

Quinces and pears give applesauce a subtle perfume, and quinces turn it rosy pink. Add 2 finely chopped peeled quinces or 3 peeled sliced pears to apples and cook. There's no reason not to combine all three fruits in a single exotic sauce.

WALNUT PANCAKES
WITH CRANBERRY SYRUP

Servings: 2–3

The combination of cranberries and walnuts make these easy-to-make pancakes a wonderfully satisfying cold-weather breakfast.

1/2 cup flour
1 tbs. sugar
1/4 tsp. baking soda
1/4 tsp. salt
1/4 tsp. cinnamon
1/2 cup toasted chopped walnuts
1/2 cup + 2 tbs. buttermilk
1 egg
1 tbs. butter, melted
1/2 cup maple syrup
1/2 cup fresh cranberries

In a bowl, stir together flour, sugar, baking soda, salt, cinnamon and walnuts. In a small bowl stir together buttermilk, egg and butter. Add buttermilk mixture to flour mixture and stir until just combined. Batter will be lumpy.

Heat a skillet over medium heat and lightly coat with butter. Pour 1/4 cup batter per pancake into skillet and cook until bubbles burst on surface and undersides are golden brown, 1 to 2 minutes. Turn and cook until golden. Keep warm in a 200° oven while you repeat with remaining batter, adding butter to pan if necessary. Serve pancakes with *Cranberry Syrup.*

CRANBERRY SYRUP

In a small saucepan, combine syrup with cranberries. Simmer, covered, for 5 minutes, or until cranberries have burst. Cover and keep warm.

SOURDOUGH PANCAKES

Start these simple, easy pancakes the night before.

1½ cups all-purpose flour
1½ tsp. active dry yeast
2 cups milk, divided
1 tsp. baking soda
2 tbs. hot water

1 cup all-purpose flour
1 egg, lightly beaten
½ tsp. salt
1 tsp. sugar
1 tbs. butter, melted

Blend together flour, yeast and 1 cup of the milk in a bowl. Cover loosely and set aside in a warm place overnight.

In the morning, whisk ½ cup of the remaining milk into starter. Dissolve baking soda in hot water. Add to starter with 1 cup flour, egg, salt, sugar, butter and remaining milk, whisking until mixture is combined. Heat a skillet over medium heat and lightly coat with oil. Pour ¼ cup batter per pancake and cook until bubbles burst on surface, 1 to 2 minutes. Turn and cook for 1 minute, or until golden. Keep warm in oven while cooking. Add oil to pan if necessary.

BROWN SUGAR BLUEBERRY PANCAKES

Servings: 3–4

A touch of lemon zest brings out the sweetness in the berries. Use frozen unsweetened blueberries if fresh are not in season.

1 egg	$3/4$ cup + 1 tbs. flour
1 tbs. grated lemon zest	1 tsp. baking powder
$3/4$ cup milk	$1/2$ tsp. salt
3 tbs. dark brown sugar, packed	1 cup fresh blueberries
2 tbs. butter, melted	

In a bowl, blend egg, lemon zest, milk, sugar and butter. In another bowl, blend flour, baking powder and salt. Stir into milk mixture until batter is just combined. Stir in blueberries.

Heat a skillet over medium-high heat and lightly coat with butter. Pour $1/3$ cup batter per pancake into skillet and cook pancakes for 2 minutes on each side, or until golden. Keep warm in a 200° oven while you repeat with remaining batter, adding butter to pan if necessary.

GINGERBREAD PANCAKES

Gingerbread pancakes, scented with spices, are great for Sunday brunch. These pancakes are like having cake for breakfast! Serve with warmed maple syrup.

3 cups flour
1 cup dark brown sugar, packed
1 tbs. baking powder
1 1/2 tsp. baking soda
1 tsp. salt
1 tsp. cinnamon
1 tsp. ground ginger
1/4 tsp. ground nutmeg

1/8 tsp. ground cloves
1/2 cup water
1/2 cup brewed coffee, cold
4 eggs
1/2 cup butter, melted and
  cooled
1/4 cup fresh lemon juice
vegetable oil for pan

In a bowl, blend together flour, brown sugar, baking powder, baking soda, salt, cinnamon, ginger, nutmeg and cloves. Whisk together water, coffee, eggs, butter and lemon juice in another bowl. Add flour mixture and whisk until just combined. Set aside for 15 minutes. Batter will thicken.

Lightly coat a large skillet with oil and heat over medium heat until hot but not smoking. Pour 1/4 cup batter per pancake into hot skillet. Cook until bubbles burst on surface and undersides are golden brown, 1 to 2 minutes. Turn pancakes and cook until cooked through and edges are lightly browned, 1 to 2 minutes longer. Keep warm in a 200° oven while you repeat with remaining batter, adding oil to pan if necessary.

BAKED SUNDAY PANCAKE
WITH RASPBERRY SAUCE

Servings: 3–4

This delightful baked pancake is also known as a Dutch baby. The pancake puffs up while it is baking but sinks down when removed from the oven. As well as Raspberry Sauce, *you could also top the pancake with confectioners' sugar and a squeeze of lemon, if you like.*

3 tbs. butter
3 eggs
3/4 cup milk
1/2 tsp. vanilla extract

1/2 cup flour
2 tbs. sugar
1/8 tsp. salt
Raspberry Sauce, page 43

Heat oven to 425°. Melt butter in a 10-inch ovenproof skillet over low heat. Remove skillet from heat and set aside.

In a large bowl, using a mixer, or in a blender container, beat or blend eggs until light and pale. Beat or blend in milk, vanilla, flour, sugar and salt.

Pour batter into prepared skillet and bake until pancake is puffed and lightly browned, 15 to 20 minutes. Slice into wedges and serve immediately with *Raspberry Sauce*.

RASPBERRY SAUCE
Makes 1 1/4 cups

4 cups fresh raspberries, or thawed frozen
2–3 tbs. sugar, or more to taste

In a food processor workbowl or blender container, blend raspberries until smooth. Strain puree into a bowl and discard seeds. Stir sugar into raspberry puree; taste and add more sugar if desired.

BAKED APPLE PANCAKES

Because these pancakes are turned in the middle of baking they have to be made in smaller skillets. They are tasty and create their own sweet sauce as they bake, so no syrup is needed.

1 Granny Smith apple, peeled, cut into slices
2 tsp. fresh lemon juice
4 eggs
¾ cup whole milk
¾ cup flour

1 tbs. + ¼ cup sugar, divided
¼ tsp. salt
¼ cup dark brown sugar, packed
1¼ tsp. cinnamon
¼ cup (½ stick) butter

In a bowl, toss apple slices with lemon juice.

In another bowl, whisk eggs and milk in a large bowl until combined. Add flour, 1 tbs. of the sugar and salt; whisk until just combined. Batter will be lumpy.

Mix brown sugar, cinnamon and remaining ¼ cup sugar in a small bowl; set aside.

Heat oven to 450°. Melt 1 tbs. of the butter in each of two 6-inch ovenproof nonstick skillets over medium heat. Pour half of the batter into each skillet. Arrange half of the apple slices evenly over batter in each skillet. Transfer skillets to oven and bake until pancakes are set around the edges but still wet in the center, about 8 minutes.

Remove from oven; sprinkle half of the brown sugar mixture over each pancake. Dot each with 1 tbs. of the butter. Using a spatula, carefully turn pancakes over.

Bake until pancakes rise, sugar mixture melts to sauce consistency, and top of pancakes is golden, about 6 minutes. Invert onto plates. Serve warm.

APPLE-WALNUT PANCAKES
WITH FUDGE SAUCE

Servings: 5–6

These are like crêpes. You can prepare most of the recipe ahead of time and assemble just before serving. Remember, cream whips best when it is very cold.

2 lb. tart apples
2 tbs. butter
1/3 cup pure maple syrup
1/2 cup chopped walnuts
1 tsp. cinnamon
1 tsp. fresh lemon juice
1/4 cup Grand Marnier orange
   liqueur

12 *Orange Pancakes*, page 48
1/2 cup heavy cream
2 tbs. confectioners' sugar
1/2 tsp. cinnamon
1/2 cup *Crème Fraîche*, page 74,
   or sour cream
1/2 cup purchased fudge sauce

Peel and core apples and cut into 1/4-inch wedges. In a skillet heat butter over medium-high heat until foam subsides. Sauté apples until golden, 6 to 8 minutes. Reduce heat to low. Carefully stir in syrup, walnuts, cinnamon and lemon juice. Cook until apples are tender but not mushy and liquid is reduced to a syrup-like consistency. Remove skillet from heat and stir in Grand Marnier. Return to low heat and cook for 1 minute, to blend flavors. Filling may be made 1 day ahead and refrigerated, covered. Reheat filling before proceeding.

Put about 2½ tbs. warm apple filling in the center of each pancake. Roll up pancakes tightly to enclose filling and place in a baking pan. Place in a 200° oven to keep pancakes warm while you make *Cinnamon Cream*. Put 2 filled pancakes on each of 6 dessert plates. Top with *Cinnamon Cream* and drizzle with fudge sauce.

CINNAMON CREAM

In a bowl, beat cream with confectioners' sugar and cinnamon until it holds soft peaks. Fold in *Crème Fraîche*.

ORANGE PANCAKES

These pancakes can be made ahead and refrigerated. Frozen, they will keep for 2 weeks.

1½ cups milk
2 tbs. Grand Marnier orange liqueur
2 tbs. butter, melted
5 eggs
1 cup flour
¼ cup sugar
1 tbs. grated orange zest
1 tsp. grated lemon zest

Mix milk, Grand Marnier, butter and eggs in a bowl until well combined. Add flour gradually. Stir in sugar, orange zest and lemon zest and refrigerate, covered, for 30 minutes.

Gently stir batter. Heat a small nonstick skillet over medium heat until hot and lightly coat with butter. When butter starts to bubble, remove pan from heat. Pour about 2 tbs. batter into skillet, tilting and rotating pan quickly to evenly coat bottom.

Return pan to heat and cook pancake until golden brown, about 1 minute. Turn pancake and cook until other side is golden brown, 1 minute longer. Remove to a plate with a paper towel between each pancake. Repeat with remaining batter, adding butter to pan if necessary.

Wrap pancakes layered with paper towels in foil. Heat foil packet in a 300° oven for about 15 minutes.

CRISPY TRADITIONAL POTATO PANCAKES

Servings: 4–6

Potato pancakes, also called latkes, are a traditional Jewish dish, but they are also found in France. For thin, crisp potato pancakes, squeeze as much liquid as possible from the shredded potato.

2 lb. russet or Yukon gold
   potatoes
1 medium onion
1/2 cup chopped scallions, white
   and green parts

1 egg, beaten
salt and pepper to taste

Peel potatoes. Using a grater or food processor, coarsely shred potatoes and onion. Place in a fine-mesh strainer or tea towel and press or squeeze out all the liquid over a bowl. The potato starch will settle to the bottom as a thick white paste.

Carefully pour off liquid in the bowl, reserving potato starch. Mix potatoes and onion with potato starch. Add scallions, egg, salt and pepper and mix well.

Heat a large skillet over medium heat and lightly coat with oil. For each pancake, take about 2 tbs. of the potato mixture in the palm of your hand and form into a flattened ball. Place in skillet, flatten with a large spatula and cook for a few minutes until golden. Flip pancake over and brown other side. Remove to paper towels to drain. Keep warm in a 200° oven while you repeat with remaining potato mixture, adding oil to pan if necessary. You can also freeze these pancakes and crisp them up in a 350° oven.

Variation: If you want a more traditional, thicker pancake, add an extra egg plus 1/3 cup of matzoh meal to the batter.

POTATO PANCAKES WITH SCALLIONS AND SMOKED MOZZARELLA

Servings: 4

These pancakes have the consistency of mashed potatoes on the inside but are crispy on the outside. Since the potatoes are already cooked, the pancakes cook quickly. Serve with a dollop of Crème Fraîche, *page 74.*

2 lb. potatoes, unpeeled
3 scallions, thinly sliced
1/2 tsp. salt
1/8 tsp. pepper
1 egg, beaten
2 tbs. *Crème Fraîche*, page 74, or sour cream
1/2 cup shredded smoked mozzarella cheese

Place potatoes in a pot of cold water over high heat and bring to a boil. Lower heat to medium and simmer, uncovered, until they're tender but not quite cooked through. Cool slightly and peel.

Coarsely shred potatoes with a box grater or the grating disc of a food processor. Toss potatoes and scallions together in a large bowl and add salt and pepper. In a small bowl, beat egg and *Crème Fraîche* together; mix into potatoes. Add cheese and mix together.

Form into cakes about 3 to 4 inches in diameter and $1/2$ inch thick. Cook in a lightly oiled skillet over medium heat until crisp and golden underneath, about 4 to 5 minutes. Flip and cook for another 4 to 5 minutes. Keep warm in a 200° oven while you repeat with remaining potato mixture, adding oil to pan if necessary.

LEEK, POTATO AND CHEESE PANCAKES

Servings: 4–5

The combination of potatoes, leeks and cheese is delicious. I use Asiago, but any melting cheese is equally appetizing. The potato mixture keeps well in the refrigerator for a day or two. Serve with a dollop of sour cream or Crème Fraîche, *page 74.*

2 lb. yellow or red skin potatoes
1 tbs. olive oil
2 medium leeks, white part only
salt and pepper
2 tsp. minced garlic

2 eggs
2 tbs. *Crème Fraîche, page 74*
¾ cup shredded fontina cheese
1½ tbs. flour
oil for the pan

Place potatoes in a pot of cold water over high heat and bring to a boil. Lower heat to medium and simmer, uncovered, until they're tender but not quite cooked through, about 25 minutes. Drain and set aside to cool.

Meanwhile, split leeks lengthwise, rinse well and slice thinly. Peel potatoes and shred with a box grater or with the grating disc of a food processor.

Heat olive oil in a medium skillet and add leeks, ¼ tsp. salt and a few pinches of pepper. Cook over medium heat until leeks begin to soften, about 3 minutes. Add garlic and cook for 1 minute longer, adding 1 to 2 tsp. water if needed to keep leeks from sticking to pan.

Combine leeks, potatoes, ½ tsp. salt and a pinch of pepper in a bowl. Beat eggs and *Crème Fraîche* together in a small bowl and stir into potatoes along with cheese and flour.

Form into little cakes about 3 to 4 inches in diameter and ½ inch thick. Cook in a well-oiled skillet over medium heat, until cakes crisp and turn golden, about 5 minutes per side. Keep warm in a 200° oven while you repeat with remaining potato mixture, adding oil to pan if necessary.

POTATO PANCAKES WITH GOAT CHEESE

Servings: 4

This dish, an unusual appetizer or vegetarian entrée, is an easy-to-make California twist on traditional potato latkes. Serve it with this simple green salad

2 russet potatoes
1/2 tsp. salt
1/4 tsp. pepper
4 oz. goat cheese, crumbled
1 tbs. wine vinegar or balsamic
  vinegar
1/2 tsp. Dijon mustard

3 tbs. olive oil
3 tbs. + 1 tsp. minced fresh
  chives, divided
1 tbs. minced shallot
1 clove garlic, minced
4 cups mixed green salad

Peel potatoes. Using a box grater or the grating disc of a food processor, shred potatoes. Place in a kitchen towel and squeeze to remove as much moisture as possible. Transfer potatoes to a large bowl. Add salt and pepper and toss to combine.

Whisk vinegar and mustard in a small bowl. Gradually whisk in oil. Mix in 2 tbs. of the chives, shallot and garlic. Season to taste with salt and pepper. Place greens in a large bowl. Set greens and dressing aside.

Heat a large heavy skillet over medium heat and lightly coat with oil. Mound 1/3 cup potatoes in skillet. Using a spatula, flatten to a 3-inch round. Repeat 3 times, forming 4 pancakes. Top each cake with 1/4 of the goat cheese. Sprinkle each cake with 1 tsp. chives. Cover each with another 1/3 cup potatoes; press to adhere, enclosing cheese completely and flattening cakes slightly. Cook until bottoms are golden, about 6 minutes. Add 1 to 2 tsp. oil to skillet and carefully turn pancakes over. Cook until golden, about 6 minutes longer.

Toss greens with reserved dressing. Divide salad among plates. Arrange 1 pancake atop each salad.

SWEET POTATO PANCAKES

Servings: 4–5

You can prepare these pancakes up to six hours ahead, leaving only a quick frying before serving. Try serving them with caviar for a really elegant appetizer!

2 lb. sweet potatoes
4–5 chopped scallions
2 eggs
1½ tbs. flour
1½ tsp. salt

½ tsp. pepper
3 tbs. (or more) vegetable oil
1 cup sour cream
chopped fresh chives for garnish

Cook sweet potatoes in a large pot of boiling salted water until just tender but still firm, about 15 minutes. Drain and refrigerate until cold, at least 2 hours, or overnight.

Peel potatoes and, using a grater or food processor, coarsely shred potatoes into a large bowl. Stir in scallions. Whisk eggs, flour, salt and pepper together in a small bowl. Gently mix into potato mixture. Form into about 48 small balls.

Heat 3 tbs. oil in a large nonstick skillet over medium-high heat. Place 8 potato balls in skillet, pressing each gently with spatula to flatten to 1½-inch diameter. Cook until pancakes are rich golden brown, about 2 minutes per side. Transfer to paper towels to drain. Keep warm in a 200° oven while you repeat with remaining potato balls, adding more oil to skillet as necessary. Transfer pancakes to a platter. Top each with 1 tsp. sour cream and garnish with chives. Serve warm or at room temperature.

CORN AND ONION PANCAKES

Servings: 4–6

These cakes are very sweet, just like fresh corn. Try whatever cheese you like in place of cheddar. You can add other herbs, or chop and add some chiles to make it spicy and Southwestern.

1/2 tbs. olive oil
1/2 medium yellow onion, diced
2 scallions, sliced, white and
    green parts separated
1/2 tsp. minced garlic
1/4 tsp. salt
1 pinch black pepper
3 cups fresh corn, or frozen,
    thawed

1/4 cup water
2 eggs, separated
8 oz. ricotta cheese
1/2 cup milk
3/4 cup shredded cheddar or
    other cheese
3 tbs. shredded Parmesan
1/2 cup flour
1 tsp. baking powder

Heat olive oil in a skillet. Add onions, white parts of scallions, garlic, salt and pepper. Sauté over medium heat until onions begin to soften, about 3 minutes. Add corn and water, lower heat and cover pan. Simmer until corn is tender, about 5 minutes. Transfer to a bowl with any remaining liquid. Add scallion greens and set aside to cool.

Combine egg yolks, ricotta, milk, cheddar and Parmesan in a bowl. Stir in corn mixture, flour, baking powder, 1/4 tsp. salt and a pinch of pepper. In another bowl, beat egg whites with a pinch of salt until stiff and gently fold them into batter.

Coat a large skillet with oil and place over medium-high heat. Pour 1/4 cup batter per pancake into skillet. Cook for about 3 minutes on each side, until cakes are golden. Keep warm in a 200° oven while you repeat with remaining batter, adding oil to pan if necessary.

BUTTERMILK CORNCAKES
WITH BELL PEPPER SALSA

Servings: 4–5

These pancakes are great for wrapping: use them to wrap some ricotta for breakfast, or fill them with sautéd fruit to make a great dessert. Top them with sour cream.

1 cup boiling water
3/4 cup cornmeal
2 eggs, beaten
1 1/2 cups buttermilk
1/2 stick butter, melted, or oil

1/4 tsp. salt
2 tsp. baking powder
1/2 tsp. baking soda
1 cup flour
Bell Pepper Salsa, page 63

In a medium bowl, whisk boiling water with cornmeal until smooth and set aside to cool for 10 minutes. Stir in eggs, buttermilk and butter, then whisk in salt, baking powder, baking soda and flour.

Lightly coat a nonstick skillet with oil and place over medium heat. Pour 1/4 cup batter per pancake into skillet. Immediately bubbles will form on the surface. Turn once, as soon as cakes begin to look a little dry on top. Cook second side until golden. Keep warm in a 200° oven and repeat with remaining batter, adding oil to pan if necessary. Top each cake with a dab of sour cream and a spoonful of *Bell Pepper Salsa*.

BELL PEPPER SALSA

Makes about 1 cup

1 tomato, finely chopped
1/2 red bell pepper, finely diced
1/2 yellow bell pepper, finely diced
2 green onions, thinly sliced

3 tbs. chopped fresh parsley
2 tsp. chopped fresh marjoram, or 1/2 tsp. dried
salt and pepper to taste
1 dash vinegar

Combine ingredients in a small bowl. Adjust seasoning and add more vinegar if necessary. Serve relish on the day you make it.

BEET AND CARROT PANCAKES

Servings: 4–5

These unusual, colorful pancakes make a great side dish or entrée.

2–3 beets, peeled and coarsely shredded

2–3 carrots, peeled and coarsely shredded

1/2 medium onion, diced

1 egg

1/2 tsp. salt

1/4 tsp. pepper

1/4 cup flour

sour cream for garnish

Combine beets, carrots and onion in a large bowl. Blend in egg, salt, pepper and flour, and stir until blended. Lightly oil a large skillet over medium heat. Pour 1/3 cup batter per pancake into skillet. Flatten each into a 3-inch round. Cook until brown and cooked through, about 4 minutes per side. Keep warm in a 200° oven while you repeat with remaining batter, adding oil to pan if necessary. Serve with sour cream.

OKONOMIYAKI (JAPANESE PANCAKES)

Servings: 4–5

This Japanese word means, 'whatever you like': so, in place of chicken, try shredded pork, beef, fish, or even chopped shrimp.

½ head Chinese cabbage
1 large carrot, shredded
½ medium onion, thinly sliced
3 stalks celery, thinly sliced
½ cup shredded cooked chicken

2 cups flour
1 egg, beaten
2 tbs. brown sugar, packed
1 tsp. salt
1 can (12 oz.) evaporated milk

In a bowl, shred cabbage; combine with carrot, onion, celery and chicken. In a separate bowl, whisk together flour, egg, brown sugar, salt and evaporated milk. Whisk in water, 1 tbs. at a time, until batter has consistency of heavy cream. Add vegetables to batter. Lightly oil a skillet over medium heat. Pour ¼ cup batter per pancake. Cook until golden brown on each side. Keep warm in a 200° oven while you cook pancakes. Add oil to pan if necessary.

SPINACH, GOAT CHEESE AND MUSHROOM PANCAKES

Servings: 4–6

These are very hearty, as appetizers or entrées. Serve with Fresh Tomato Salsa, *page 75,* Crème Fraîche, *page 74, or sour cream.*

8 cups fresh spinach, packed
2 tbs. olive oil, divided
1/2 lb. shiitake mushrooms,
   stems discarded, sliced
salt and pepper
3 cloves garlic, finely chopped
2 scallions, thinly sliced

2 eggs, separated
8 oz. ricotta cheese
1/2 cup milk
1/2 cup flour
1 tsp. baking powder
2 oz. goat cheese, crumbled

Rinse spinach well and remove large stems; set aside. Heat 1 tbs. of the olive oil in a large skillet and add mushrooms, 1/4 tsp. salt and a few pinches of pepper. Sauté over medium heat for 3 to 5 minutes. Add garlic and scallions and cook for 1 to 2 minutes longer. Transfer to a bowl.

Return skillet to heat and add spinach, remaining 1 tbs. olive oil, $\frac{1}{8}$ tsp. salt and a few pinches of pepper. Cook spinach in batches if necessary. When spinach is wilted, squeeze dry, chop coarsely and add to mushroom mixture.

In a small bowl, using a whisk or mixer, beat egg whites to stiff peaks. In a medium bowl, combine egg yolks, ricotta and milk. Stir in flour, baking powder, $\frac{1}{4}$ tsp. salt and a pinch of pepper. Stir vegetables and goat cheese into batter; fold in egg whites.

Lightly oil a skillet and place over medium-high heat. Pour $\frac{1}{4}$ cup batter per pancake into skillet. Cook on each side for about 3 minutes until browned, turning cakes only once. Do not flatten with a spatula. Keep warm in a 200° oven while you repeat with remaining batter, adding oil to pan if necessary.

LEEK AND BACON PANCAKES

This is a baked savory pancake, similar to a frittata.

2 large leeks, white parts only	1/2 cup flour
8 slices bacon	1 tbs. Dijon mustard
3 eggs	1/2 tsp. sugar
3/4 cup milk	1 cup shredded Gouda, packed

Split leeks lengthwise, rinse well, chop and set aside. In an oven-proof skillet, cook bacon over medium-high heat until brown and crisp. Drain on paper towels. Crumble bacon. Pour off all but 2 tbs. of the bacon drippings from skillet. Add leeks and sauté over medium heat until tender and beginning to brown, about 8 minutes. Combine eggs, milk, flour, mustard and sugar in a food processor; blend until smooth. Season with salt and pepper. Add bacon to leeks in skillet. Pour egg mixture over. Sprinkle Gouda on top. Heat oven to 425°. Transfer to oven and bake until pancake puffs and cheese melts, about 15 minutes. Cut into wedges and serve.

BELL PEPPER AND CILANTRO PANCAKES

Servings: 4–6

Serve these colorful, delicate pancakes at room temperature.

²/₃ cup flour
¹/₄ cup cornmeal
¹/₂ tsp. red pepper flakes
²/₃ cup milk
¹/₂ cup diced bell pepper

3 tbs. chopped fresh cilantro
2 eggs, separated
sour cream for garnish
5 oz. smoked salmon, in strips
fresh cilantro for garnish

In a bowl, stir together flour, cornmeal, pepper flakes, milk, bell pepper, cilantro and egg yolks. Add salt and pepper to taste. In another bowl, beat egg whites until they just hold stiff peaks. Gently fold into batter. Heat a skillet over medium heat and lightly coat with butter. Pour 1 tbs. batter per pancake into skillet. Cook until bubbles burst on surface and underside is golden brown, about 1 minute. Turn and cook until golden. Transfer to a rack to cool.

Garnish with sour cream, smoked salmon, and cilantro.

GREEN ONION AND CILANTRO PANCAKES

Servings: 4–6

These pancakes are influenced by the green onion cakes popular in China. Find rice flour in Asian grocery stores, or simply use 1 cup all-purpose flour.

1 tsp. sesame seeds
1/3 cup soy sauce
2 tbs. rice vinegar
1/2 tsp. sesame oil
3/4 cup all-purpose flour
1/4 cup rice flour
1/2 tsp. salt
1 egg

1 egg yolk
1 cup water
1 small green Thai or serrano
   chile, seeded and minced
1/8 tsp. pepper
1/8 tsp. sesame oil
4 green onions, chopped
1/4 cup fresh cilantro leaves

Toast seeds in a small skillet over medium-low heat just until golden. Stir together soy sauce, vinegar and sesame oil in a small bowl, then stir in sesame seeds. Set sauce aside.

Whisk together flours, salt, egg, egg yolk, water, chile, pepper and sesame oil in a bowl. Batter will be thin. Lightly coat an 8-inch nonstick skillet with oil and place over medium-high heat until hot but not smoking. Pour in 1/3 cup batter, then scatter 1/4 of the scallions and 1/4 of the cilantro leaves over top, gently pressing into pancake. Cook pancake until underside is pale golden, about 2 minutes. Turn over and cook until scallions are lightly browned, about 1 minute longer. Keep warm in a 200° oven while you repeat with remaining batter, scallions and cilantro, adding oil to pan after each batch. There may be some leftover batter.

Transfer pancakes to a cutting board and cut each into 8 wedges. Serve warm or at room temperature, with a dipping sauce.

ZUCCHINI PANCAKES WITH HERB CREAM

Because of their moisture and texture, zucchini make wonderful savory pancakes.

¾ cup sour cream
2 tbs. water
¼ cup chopped fresh basil
2 tbs. chopped fresh chives
½ tsp. salt
4 cups coarsely shredded
   zucchini

1½ tsp. salt
¼ cup flour
1½ tsp. sugar
¼ tsp. black pepper
2 egg whites

To make *Herb Cream,* p lace sour cream, water, basil, chives and ½ tsp. salt in a blender container and process until smooth and pale green. Refrigerate until ready to serve.

To remove excess moisture from grated zucchini, place in a colander and toss with 1½ tsp. salt. Set aside for 20 minutes, then squeeze zucchini in a kitchen towel to wring out as much liquid as possible. Transfer to a large bowl and stir in flour, sugar and pepper.

In a separate bowl, using a whisk or mixer, beat egg whites until they just hold stiff peaks, then gently fold into zucchini mixture.

Place a 10-inch nonstick skillet over medium-high heat, coat with oil and heat until hot but not smoking. Pour 2 tbs. batter per pancake into skillet, flattening slightly with back of a spoon. Cook pancakes, turning once, until golden brown, about 3 minutes total, transferring to paper towels to drain. Keep warm in a 200° oven while you repeat with remaining batter, adding more oil to skillet as necessary. Serve immediately with reserved *herb cream.*

CRÈME FRAÎCHE

This is similar to sour cream (which can be used as a substitute), but is richer and has a distinctive tang. It keeps for weeks in the refrigerator. It is suggested in lots of recipes in this book. You can buy crème fraîche, but it is worth making your own.

1 pint heavy cream
1 tbs. buttermilk

Pour heavy cream into a jar or plastic container, add buttermilk and whisk together. Set container in a warm place in the kitchen (on top of the refrigerator is a good spot) and place a lid on top, but leave it ajar to help the culture grow. Cream will thicken after 24 hours and you can use it at this point, but leaving it for another 12 hours is even better. Then cover and refrigerate.

FRESH TOMATO SALSA

This easy salsa is great in the summer, when tomatoes are sweet and juicy. Yellow and red tomatoes make it bright and colorful. Use lime instead of wine vinegar if you like.

$1/4$ cup diced red onion
1 tbs. wine vinegar
1 lb. tomatoes, cored and chopped
2 jalapeño chiles, seeded and finely diced
2 tbs. coarsely chopped fresh cilantro
$1/4$ tsp. salt

Sprinkle onion with vinegar, then toss with tomatoes, chiles, cilantro and $1/4$ tsp. salt. Season to taste with more salt and vinegar, if necessary. For a hotter salsa, add more chiles or include some of the seeds from the jalapeño.

INDEX